Hans-Martin Sass

Health and Happiness of Political Bodies

Hans-Martin Sass

HEALTH AND HAPPINESS OF POLITICAL BODIES

Biocultures, Businesses, Biopolitics

LIT

Cover images:
Front: The frontispiece of the book Leviathan
by Thomas Hobbes; engraving by Abraham Bosse
https://de.wikipedia.org/wiki/Datei:Leviathan_by
_Thomas_Hobbes.jpg)
Back: H. M. Sass (private)

This book is printed on acid-free paper.

Bibliographic information published by the Deutsche Nationalbibliothek
The Deutsche Nationalbibliothek lists this publication in the Deutsche Nationalbibliografie; detailed bibliographic data are available in the Internet at http://dnb.dnb.de.

ISBN 978-3-643-91305-0 (pb)
ISBN 978-3-643-96305-5 (PDF)

A catalogue record for this book is available from the British Library.

Flössergasse 10
CH-8001 Zürich
Tel. +41 (0) 76-632 84 35
E-Mail: zuerich@lit-verlag.ch http://www.lit-verlag.ch
Distribution:
In the UK: Global Book Marketing, e-mail: mo@centralbooks.com
In North America: Independent Publishers Group
e-mail: orders@ipgbook.com
In Germany: LIT Verlag Fresnostr. 2, D-48159 Münster
Tel. +49 (0) 2 51-620 32 22, Fax +49 (0) 2 51-922 60 99,
e-mail: vertrieb@lit-verlag.de

Content

INTRODUCTION

This lecture about interactions and integrations of biology, bioethics, biopolitics, bioecologies and biocultures of political bodies was presented 2019 at a joint conference of the European Academy of Arts and Sciences and the German-Japanese Society of Integrated Sciences in Salzburg, under the title 'Biocomplexity, Bioethics and Integration'. In this extended publication, sections 3 and 5 include discussions on 'homo faber and homo ludens' from a presentation in Seoul 2019 and on 'special risks' from my book 'Cultures in Bioethics' 2016. In order to preserve the format of a lecture, publication numbers following names refer to endnote resources. The concluding narrative 'the little town by the river' was influenced by the prophet Mohamed's 'Contract of Medina' and discusses a stable political body connected by various networks of trade and communication in a pluralistic harmonious society leaving controversial ideological topics to future debates.

In 1926, the German pastor Fritz Jahr in Halle coined the term 'Bioethik' and defined a 'Bio-Ethical Imperative: Respect every living being as an end in itself and treat it, if possible, as such'. Bioethics since then has grown from medical ethics and social and political strategies to multidisciplinary and integrated disciplines of research and consulting. In 2020, reflecting and mediating the interactive and integrated ecosystems and interactive networks in biology, society, business, technology and communication, I submit a wider integrated biocultural, corporate and political 'Bio-Cultural Imperative: Support direct human inter-action and common-sense as an end in itself and use hardware and software tools only in stabilizing healthy and happy cultures in the bodies of ecologies, corporations and politics'.

In 1989 the Berlin Wall fell down, in 1993 the World Trade Center in New York fell down, in 2020 a global Corona pandemic fell down on people and communities. Biological, political and corporate bodies chance, and we change with them and in them: 'tempora mutantur et nos mutamur in illis'.

Reston, Virginia, USA,
Hans-Martin Sass

1

BIOS IS INTEGRATED, COMPLEX, AND ADAPABLE

Bios is complex and it is integrated. The cells of my body are complex in their DNA, have a metabolism of their own and interact with other cells and organs; cells of blood, skin, liver, brain and other organs are different. I cannot live alone; I have a father and a mother, friends and foes, neighbors, colleagues, and other networks. I need the microbes in my intestine to co-digest foods and drinks for their and my health, happiness, and my and their good and long life. My genetic heritage of active and dormant chromosomes comes from the interaction and recombination of my father's and my mother's DNA, but then modifies somewhat in epigenetic interaction with my mother's body and even after birth depending on the biotope.– My body has about 30 trillion cells and is closely integrated with roughly 100 trillion microbes, keeping each other alive (Money 2012) The very personal genetic codes of my DNA and RNA integrate five different nucleobases ACGTU (adenine, cystine, guanine, thymine, uracil) and additional bases, which have been formed after my nucleoid acid chain has formed. I share these integrated and interacting bases with all forms of life, which actually differentiate bios from non-bios. Physics and astrophysics inform us about integrations, interactions, interferences among protons, atoms, molecules, planets, milky ways and multiverses.

Individual and collective bios displays a certain 'groupiness' expressed by species-specific and individual-specific degrees of the 8 C's capacities: 'communication and cooperation, competency and competition, contemplation and calculation, compassion and cultivation' (Sass 2016:45ff). Of course, the 8 C's represent themselves species-specific in different arrangements and representations. But even the most primitive one-cell archaea with no specific cell-skin or nucleus and minimal DNA can 'smell' and move towards foods, also 'tell' other archaea about the direction towards foods. 'Variatio delectat' said the old Romans; diversity is enjoyable, but it is also indispensable for a stable and strong bios.

Biology as a narrowly defined natural science studies these 8 C's and their differentiations in individuals, species, and biotopes. But the world of bios is larger than traditional biology; it covers all complex adaptable systems (CAS) of natural and cultural biotopes, and of political and corporate bodies. Here is a definition of CAS, which does not come from traditional biology, but from social science and economic theory: 'Complex adaptive systems are often nested in broader systems. A population is a CAS nested in a naturel ecosystem, which in itself is nested in the broader biological environment. A company is a CAS nested in a business ecosystem, which is nested in the broad societal environment. Complexity therefore exists at multiple levels, not just within the organizational boundaries; and at each level there is tension between what is good for an individual agent and what is good for the larger system'. (Reeves 2016).

The 64 hexagrams of the mythical Emperor-Dragon Fu Xi, over 3000 years ago, describe these integrated complexities not just in nature but in individual humans, families, communities, society, ecosystems. Confucius' slogan 'in harmony, different, not identical (君子和而不同) he er bu tong, Lin Yu 13:2 (Zhai 2011) describes a similar integrated and integrating bios, which hopefully succeeds in social harmony, also the 'e pluribus unum' (one made out of many) the motto of the first 13 states of the USA. Much earlier was the old Vedic wisdom 'tat tvam asi – this is also you', i.e. the dying or blooming flower, the tigress and her cubs, the snake, the suffering fellow-human, any other creature. The Tat Tvam Asi is not just a biological information, it also holds an essential bioethical message and request 'do not harm', or as the prayer of Adi Sankara holds: 'May all be happy, may all be free from disease; may all look for the good of others; may no one suffer' (Kishore 2007:94). Buddhist reasoning, especially in the Mahayana tradition, has focused on 'the means-to and meanings-of liberating patterns of interdependence, based on the insight that relationality is ontologically primary and that relational dynamics are always open to significant improvements' (Hershock 2012). Carolingian King Lothar described the complex interaction and integration of individuals with their political and social biotopes as 'tempora mutantur and nos mutamur in in illis': times are changing and we change within them. Similarly, Greek philosopher Heraclites said 'you cannot go into the same river twice'. The European enlightened tradition of 'subsidiarity' holds 'that peace, respect for persons and other treasured values of a society rich in cultural and ethical values will fall apart if individual freedom is not granted ... cross-cultural ethics is a visionary enterprise and a great mission, which will fail, if the dignity of fellow-human's conscience, their vulnerability, and the principles of communication-in-trust, cooperation-in-trust, discursivity and tolerance do not form the core principles' (Sass 2003:19).

Jesus quotes the Jewish Prophet Micah when reducing the hundreds of rules and requirements in Judaic religion into the essential message 'respect God and love your neighbor as you love yourself'.

Indeed, we find this essential message in all regions and religions despite their intellectual or revelational differences. Similarly, the Prophet Mohamed in a hadith said ‘and when you hold all the requirements for Ramadan and other laws, but have no mercy with your brother, then Allah will have no merci with you!’ (Sass 2018b). The father of modern bioethics, Pastor Fritz Jahr in Halle/Saale defined a ‘Bioethical Imperative: Respect every living being as an end in itself and treat it, if possible, as such!’(Jahr 2013:20f).

2

Integrative Biology of Political Bodies

Aesop's fable of the organs rebelling against the 'lazy' belly stomach and stopping to feed him describes the biological and biopolitical integration of the body parts. Hobbes was one of the philosophers following the 'corpuscularianist school' (Newman 2006) discussing chemical elements of alchemy in interaction. In 'De Cive' 1642 he quoted the Roman slogan 'homo homini lupus', one human is the wolf of the other. Plants and trees, making up over 80% of the global biomass, do not limit themselves to one highly central brain as we and animals do, who simply can run away from threats. Some trees can live thousands of years in interaction and relative harmony with their biotope; they spread their capacities such as photosynthesis, and respiration throughout the entire body, interacting underground with microbes and other plants, recognizing and interacting above ground in competition with other bios. They are, describes neurobiologist Stefano Mancuso (2018:XIf), 'the living representation of how stability and flexibility can be combined. Their modular, diffused construction is the epitome of modernity: a cooperative, shared structure without command centers, able to flexibly resist repeated catastrophic events without losing functionality and adopt very quickly to huge environmental changes. It is no coincidence that the internet, the very symbol of modernity, is built like a root system. When it comes it robustness and flexibility, nothing can compete with plants. ... We would do well to bear this in mind when planning for our future as a species'. Dictatorships are highly centralized as Bosse's engraving of the Leviathan suggests. Some nations such as Switzerland, the USA and the FRG are 'federal republics', representing more a strong and well-integrated tree than a dictatorial man. Would it be acceptable to compare the photosynthesis from 'above', which keeps the metabolism of plants and trees alive and well, with the 'spiritual' light from above which keeps the physical and emotional metabolism of human individuals and collectives alive and well?

Interesting is the detailed analysis of the human body and the political body by the Muslim scholar Al-Farabi (2001:25:23): 'Both the city and the household have an analogy with the body of the human being. The body is composed of different parts ..., each doing a certain action, so that from all their actions they come together in mutual assistance to perfect the purpose of the human being's body. In the same way, both the city and the household are composed of different parts of a definite number ..., each performing on its own a certain action, so that from their actions they come together in mutual assistance to perfect the purpose of the city or the household'. At a 1989 conference in Bochum, Hao-Cai Liang, Director of the Department of Social Medicine, Wuhan University, presented 8 theses for integrating people's health into political bodies (Sass 2006: 413, 356): '1. For developing countries such as the Peoples Republic of China future strategies of planning should be oriented themselves toward social needs of the people not economic progress. 2. Contemporary goals of compensation of health harm need to be replaced new goals keeping people healthy as a social base. 3. Keeping health should be based more on responsible self-care of people than on medical intervention. 4. The biological model needs to be replaced by an integrated biological-psychological-social model. High-tech medicine needs to be accomplished by high levels of caring for the patient. 5. High-tech medicine and high-touch medicine belong together. 6. Not the newest available technology, but the technology most adequate for this particular patient should be used. 7. Health industry as part of economic production needs to be replaced by medicine as a part of the service sector. 8. Instead of centralizing medical activity in central hospital, decentralized ambulatory care of the patent should be favored.' Confucian scholar Sun Si Mio once said 'Superior doctors treat the state, better doctors treat a patient, common doctors treat the illness'. Following Liang's and Sun's Confucius's 8 rules of 'great learning', we can formulate: prepare for triage, natural disasters end endemics, biomedical terror and warfare; establish survivable information networks; test and control that experts and materials are ready any time; provide full and open information to experts and citizens; involve citizens and communities as partners in crisis prevention and management. As epidemics and other health risks may reach global proportions, it is a national self-interest a well as a human obligation to cooperate globally in creating a more healthy and harmonious world and to fight the spread the disease.

E. O. Wilson (1975) defines sociobiology as 'the extension of population biology and evolutionary theory to social organizations'. St Paul, probably well aware of Plato's comparison of the city with a body, describes (Colossian 1:18f) the diversity of a religious community and their interaction with Christ as 'the head of the body, the church': 'For just as the body is one and has many members, and all the members of the body, though many, are one body, so it is with Christ'. Political bodies, just as human and other bodies, have complex, integrated and interacting cells and organs.– But we humans are not perfectly eusocial as the folks of ants and bees (Cox-Foster et al 2007). These eusocial folks never had experienced something alike the French Revolution or Lenin's or Mao's toppling of existing hierarchies; nor did they experiment with various forms of sociality such as dictatorships, anarchies, democracies, meritocracies in pure or mixed form following each other and being of different life time. As Aristotle described, meritocracies can deteriorate into nepotism, democracies into anarchies, and monarchies into dictatorships. Just as my body has various different cells and organs, the political body needs bone structure, muscles, networks of blood and nerves. Being somewhat social alike wolves and cows, and more social than foxes and swans, we humans are gifted and burdened with the conflict between individual interest and group interest. Christine de Pizan, a lady writer at the Court of Charles V was the first who described a detailed anatomy and physiology of the biology of a Corps Politic (de Pizan 1407, Langdon Forham 2002).

It was Hobbes 'Leviathan or the Matter, Former and Power of Common Wealth Ecclesiastical and Civil',1651, which influenced political theory and praxis in Europe distrusting people and suggesting a strong dictatorship waving the sword in one hand and a ruler's crosier in the other, the political and social body consisting of people of different profession age and sex in front of a cultivated biotope of meadows, houses, machines, courts, castles and tanks, as the Abraham Bosse sketch in the 1651 Hamburg edition shows. Hobbes did not yet discuss benefits to health and harmony of political bodies based integrated, flexible and complex bodies of democracy as being stable strong like a good old tree. What photosynthesis does for plants, religious or other spiritual values of humans might do for the metabolism of healthy social human bodies.

3

Tool Use Cultures: Homo Faber and Homo Ludens

When our ancestors left African jungle trees a million years ago, we used sticks for clearing brushes and cuttings ways, intimidating or defeating unfriendly animals and human rivals. We learned to control fire and water as energy and developed more diverse tools such as spates and axes, nails and hammers, sheds and houses, walls and castles, wagons and ships, black power for fireworks and shooting ammunition. We also bred and crossbred cultured plants and animals such as rice, wheat, and apples, and camels, mules, dogs, horses and cows for food and commerce, and some just for company. Personal and societal experiences and ecosystems grow bigger and more complex due to our complex tool use. We humans are creating and using tools – hardware tools and software tools – and we correctly have called ourselves Homo Faber, the tool use species. – Hardware tools include hammers and axes, farms and vineyards, houses and castles, cars and mails, networks of electricity and commerce, but also toys for adults and kids.

But we humans also created software tools, for shared social use, including values, customs, laws, traditions, festivities, parties and plays. These software tools as well demonstrate a special species-capacity to build societies and networks, including rules and values, punishments and honors, Gods and Goddesses, good and evil spirits, languages and traditions, ceremonies and festivals, parties and plays. Narratives about family members, actual and deceased, imaginary dangerous or friendly spirits, gods and goddesses, devils and guardian angels, ceremonies and fests honoring the seasons, emperors, local or religious communities or corporations in multiple fashions. Thus, by using more and more complex software tools, we modified also our social biotopes from family clans and small neighborhoods to villages, cities, kingdoms and religious empires of various kind. These spiritual and social tools were formed and kept together by ever changing networks social, cultural and political composition, that included clan and neighborhood traditions, retold oral and written narratives, educational cultivation of kids and communities and the formation and boding of communities hold together by shared spiritual dreams and convictions, plays and games, ceremonies and festivals. These software tools made communities stable and prosperous by division of labor and expertise, and by enforcing legal and political tools.

The two remarkable biological properties of the human species, Contemplation and Calculation, can be documented throughout history in all cultures, empowerment of the 'sons of light battling the evils of darkness' (Ahuramazda), and uncountable variations of religions providing 'insight' of intellectual, philosophical, social, mystical, spiritual and emotional togetherness and understanding of self-identity. The virtual reality of gods, goddess, and saints in many religions has proven its real power in guiding and 'protecting' me and my loved ones from misery and evil spirits.

Most of our hardware tools are technical such as hammers, cars, phones, but others are animate tool such as plants, animals, parks and farms. Animate life needs oxygen and light, neurobiological chemicals such as oxytocin and dopamine for breathing, foods and sleep, feels love, despair and happiness. Inanimate tools feel neither despair nor love; they either are successful or unsuccessful, whether separate like a hammer or coordinated like assembly lines or algorithm processes; the need electricity or other energy working. So far, we have cultivated animate tools only indirectly by breeding and crossbreeding, selecting or killing in favor of cultivated city and agricultural ecosystems. Only recently Crispr-Cas9 technology has given us the tools to directly construct life form tools, including manipulating human life. While some traditional breeding results did potentially harm animals such as dachshunds with inherited spine vulnerabilities especially when required to use staircases or impoverish natural diversity by monoculture farming. But Crispr will increase those conflicts. – Life emotions, such as the 3 Christian virtues ‘faith, hope, love’ or the 9 reactions in tantric yoga ‘love, humor, wonder, courage, calmness, anger, sadness, fear, and disgust’, require oxytocin and dopamine, while robot companions and machine learning are powered by electricity or other non-animated energy without requiring oxytocin. Algorithms in mathematics, business and science perform self-contained and eventually self-learning step-by-step calculations, predictions and suggestions in automated reasoning. Interactive social robots such as dementia care companions hugging seniors, measuring their pulse, telling stories and playing music, other artificial empathy tools such as interactive and well programmed sex dolls become more and more part of our individual and collective environment. While my 80+ years old teddy bear formed my emotional personality, elderly care tools and sex tools open a new variety of social and emotional cultures for even more changing individual and collective diversity. ‘Neuralink’ and similar robot tools very soon will allow to direct affect brain reaction for therapeutic purposes, but also ‘brain enhancing' in a symbiosis with artificial empathy and intelligence.

How to we master healthy and happy tool use cultures? Since Cain killed his brother Abel (Gen 4:8), tools have been used and even developed for domination, torture, stealing, lying. Some tools, such as my $10 calculator, are smarter more efficient than myself; others such as learning algorithms machines may develop their own strategies, environments and applications such as Amazon, Facebook or Tencent; others tools provide exclusive limitations in block-chain applications. Algorithm tools may destroy deliberately or uncontrolled social, military or technical territories more targeted and precise than nuclear war. Public health care data will improve diagnosis and therapy but may also feed exploitation and destroy privacy. Social interactive tools change individual and societal conduct and activities.

Businesses, the media and governments may use extended powers for guidance or control. Growth National Product (GNP) figures allow for economic planning, but Gross Happiness Product (GHP) measures overall health and sustainability of political, civil, and spiritual bodies, first introduced 1972 by Jigme Singye Wangchuck, King of Bhutan is an empirical tool in political sociology, advising leaders, the public and the media on policy issues. Community happiness includes Seasonal Festivals: Spring, Moon,

Harvest, New Year, Carnival, Oktoberfests, National Holidays, Religious Holidays; Local Festivals: Kindergarten Fests, School Fests, Sport Team Fests, Neighborhood Fests, Highrise Neighbor's Parties, Local Hero Birthdays, Temple and Church Annual Fests, Private Club Fests (Bhutan 2013). The five-year plans include goals and estimates of costs in support of industry, transport, communication,, education, health, energy, trade, renewable natural resources, environment, government, vulnerable populations. In 2015 the website www.grossnationalhappiness.c om reported that 8.4% people were deeply happy, 35% extensively happy, 47.9% narrowly happy, 8.8% unhappy; this was an 1.8% improvement over the 2010 figures. Men were happier than women, people living in residential areas happier than rural people, farmers less happy than people in other occupations. The United Nations adopted the pursuit of happiness and the Gross Happiness Product as an ideal instrument to measure stability and health of a society and other political body; the UNO's slogan for 2015 was 'your happiness is part of something bigger'.

A *Human Freedom Index* (HFI), published jointly by the Cato Institute, the Frazer Institute, and the Friedrich Ebert Foundation, covers the rule of law, security and safety, movement, religion, civil society, expression, relationships, seize of government, legal system and property rights, access to sound money, freedom to trade internationally, regulation of credit, labor and business and measured personal, civil and economic freedom with Hong Kong, Switzerland, Finland, Denmark the first four and Saudi Arabia, Venezuela, Zimbabwe, Iran among the last of the 512 countries (Vasquez, Porcnik 2018).

Zhong has suggested to review classical Chinese concepts of family and family connectedness may serve as a model for new biocultures in the 21th century: 'Following the wisdom of Chinese people on family happiness could help to build a harmonious society in the world: draw on their empathy, putting themselves in others' shoes, addressing others' needs and concerns, showing love for one's nearest of kin, one's fellowmen and all living things' (Zhong 2014:152). Fan (206:214) reminds us that cultural, social and political interconnectedness in the Confucian sense does not mean equal, but rather 'differentiated and graded connectedness': '1. One has moral obligations to take care of one's family members (such as one's parents, spouse, and children), than others in one's local or religious community (such as neighbors, friends, and acquaintances); 2. One has more moral obligations to take care of those in one's local or religious community than other citizens in the state; and 3. One has moral obligation to take care of one's fellow citizen in the state than other people in other states'.

Moses Mendelsohn (1819:201), the enlightened humanist and faithful Rabbi, in 1819 argued in regard to cultural diversity and religious fighting: 'Brethren, if you want true peacefulness in God, let us not lie about consensus when plurality seemed to have been the plan and the goal of providence. No one among us reasons and feels precisely the same way the fellow human does. Why do we hide from each other in masquerades in the most important issues of our lives, as God not without reason has given each of us his/her own image and face'? Given the quest for harmony and the diverse and often contrarian powers within social, cultural and political bodies, we may we rephrase Mendelsohn's insight into the diverse bios of individual humans and human communities into a bioethical suggestion: Brethren, citizens, politicians, and leaders, if you want peace and harmony in our political life, then let us not lie about uniformity when adaptability, plurality, and modality seems to have been the blueprint in the wisdom of bios. No one among the bodies politic has a fully identical body structures and social interactions as compared to the others. Why do we hide from each other behind the masquerades of one-size-fits-all democracies or similar bodies, as the vital, interconnected, highly adaptable, diverse, and complex human bios has not without reason given us and our political bodies different shapes and shades?

Play is considered more important than school for children's social development (Sahlberg 2019). The proven historic remedy against tool domination by robots is direct human interaction in flesh, among the young, children, families, clubs, religious and other circles, sports teams, neighborhoods. Isaak Asimov's Law of Robotics (1942): 'First Law: A robot may not injure a human being, or through inaction, allow a human to come to harm. – Second Law: A robot must obey the orders given it by human beings except where such orders would conflict with the First Law. – Third Law: A robot must protect its own existence as long as such protection does not conflict with the First or Second Law, or may not injure a human being or, through inaction, allow a human being to come to harm'. Asimov also combined these three laws by a central one 'a robot may not harm humanity, or, by inaction, allow humanity to come to harm'.

4

Variations and Modifications of Political Bodies

Hegel described world history as progressively implementing individual liberty and healthy political bodies in a Eurocentric direction, guided by the 'cunning of reason': 'World history travels from east to west; for Europe is the absolute end of history, just as Asia is the beginning' (Hegel). Hegel was wrong when he declared the European culture as the final point of history, but he rightly recognized that progress in history involves passions (Leidenschaften) and powerful people such as Napoleon, who toppled the European monarchies and riding through Hegel's hometown Jena as the 'world spirit on a horse'. But then, the Vienna Congress and the restitution of the ancient regimes were the result of Napoleon's wars, and a Napoleon Bonaparte crowned himself as Emperor of France. What good did the German Extermination Camps or the Japanese Rape of Nanjing do for the progress of liberty and freedom in Europe and China, where Stalin's and Mao's cruel dictatorships followed? The narrative of 'cunning of reason' may be good as a vision, but reality is different. All complex adaptable and changing bodies of individual and collective bios need permanent modification and adaption to protect and to further develop and strengthen individual and collective bios. Humankind has made great progress in cultivating raw biotopes into cities and agricultures and inventing machines and internets of various kind. But we also use these new technologies to torture people by electricity rather than beating them with sticks and to steal via digital instruments rather than braking into houses, and to make other countries and military forces 'blind and deafen'. To cause an electric grid or other integrated systems to collapse or malfunction, one does not have to attack it directly, rather one can sneak into it via the suppliers of such systems such as was done via multiple contractors of those systems (Smith, Barry 2019).

Given the 'species-and-culture specific' human biology, our social bodies and our individual self-understandings depend on our especially strong human competence for contemplation and calculation, i.e. finding messages, posts, commandments, rules in the cyberspaces of religions, narratives, books and traditions to be implemented in our individual and collective geo-spaces. Modern cyberspace networks of individual and social bodies are more integrated and interdependent; 500 and even 50 years ago small communities could survive on their own and individuals were multi-tasking; today I depend on electricity and internets of people and expert support and supply. Artificial Emotional Intelligence today is progressing not only in devising sensitive teddy bears for demented fellow humans, but also for lonely singles providing imaginary boyfriends or girlfriends. Li (2019:22) describes the more or less intimate relationships of a single Chinese lady Ivy Deng with her imaginary boyfriends, a policeman, a scientist, a CEO and a pop star; the policeman calling her at bedtime and announcing to pick her up by motorbike the next morning to bring her to the job, but in real life he has no bike and is not a policeman, just a paid actor. Could emotional and social robots topside our traditional cultures in friendship and lovemaking?

Do sex robots performing BDSM services would violate Asimov's laws and should not be allowed (Lin 2018)? Will new interactive emotional cobots (Kline 2017), also called teledildos, replace traditional lovemaking and interactive intimacy similar to the replacement of some of my rationality by much better artificial algorithms and calculus? Will my personal sex cobot provide more emotion and love than my human girlfriend, and will she as a cobot open new experiences more satisfying than any human friend can do? Will Crispr-Cas9 technologies replace traditional baby-making by a better production of improved individual and enhanced collective human bodies and spirits? Will in-vitro meat replace chicken farms and slather houses? Will traditional wars fought with guns and soldiers be replaced by permanent stages of sabotage, manipulations, falsifications, alterations of military hardware-and software, and of digital organs of non-state and state bodies? Will teledildos and other intellectual and emotional complex robots become new 'artificial citizens' of our cities and network communities similar to 'corporate citizens' similar to Amazon, Google and Tencent? Hillis (2019) argues: 'These hybrid intelligences have superhuman powers. They can know more than individual humans; they can sense more; they can make more complicated analyses and more complex plans. They can have vastly more resources an power than any single individual... these AIs would be citizens of their nation-state in the same way that many commercial corporations often act as 'corporate citizen' today.'

AI robots don't need oxygen as we and plants and animals need, but they can provide us humans with oxytocin for bios interaction and happiness, while they themselves don't need those neurobiological substances. We are not privy to the contemplative and calculative powers of other species; my dog barks once in while in his dreams, but I don't know much about his cyberspace adventures and dependencies, if there are any. Religions have not always been supportive in building happy and healthy social bodies. They have encouraged groups and individuals to slaughter or torture fellow humans over such strange issues whether God is one-in-three or three-in-one. Religions also have encouraged monks and nuns to emigrate from their social community into orgasmic integration with imaginary saints, similar to fellow humans today addicted to cyberspace communication and cooperation in internet arcades while not meaningfully being integrated in their geo-space. Will robotic AI companions and loving cobot fellows serve similar purposes or will they even actively create new orientational and emotional networks for us as individuals and groups and cohorts. AI fellow and cohorts, of course, are much more superior of my own intellectual and calculating capacities; they will also be much better in understanding long range risks and develop good strategies to fight them. But will they also take superior control, reminding us about urgencies enthusiastically for something such as the actual corona crisis?

Facebook has 2 billion inhabitants, China only 1.4 billion; the annual budget of Alibaba, Amazon or Tencent each is higher than that of 80% of nation states. The technologies and products of Artificial Intelligence are much superior to my own rational capacities, such as my 10$ calculator does a much better job than I myself when calculating my taxes by yearend. I depend on AI and other technological companions just as I depend on the milkman and the supermarket for my daily food and drinks. Of course, this dependency involves risks which our grandfathers and grandmothers had no reason to be concerned about.

The twenty-first century has developed new scenarios of specific risk features for the survival of modern biotopes of human cultures and societies; I will mention half a dozen of these: (1) a global pandemic killing millions or billions of people, (2) an electromagnetic pulse destroying the microchip-based infrastructure of modern societies, (3) a mushrooming loss of trust in a paper-and-promise global economy, (4) local or global potentials for revolts and repressions based in digital biotopes, (5) territorial mix-up risk of being confused about geographical and cyberspace realities, and (6) loss of control risk in vast complex and changing biotopes of integrated bios in geography and cyberspace (Sass 2016:239ff).

5

Special Risks to Political and Corporate Bodies

(1) Global Pandemics and Biological Warfare: On and off, viral and bacterial infections break out naturally, mostly caused by naturally modified pathogens with different toxicities and lead times of incubation, as the global corona virus pandemic demonstrates. But human diseases have also been weaponized. Around 1000 B.C. the Hittites drove infected people into enemy's lands; in 1346 A.D. the Mongols catapulted corpses of plague victims into the Crimean city of Kaffa; during the 2nd World War the Japanese through ceramic bombs with bubonic plague fleas into the city of Ningbo. And today, different from the innocent people who happen to be victims of the Corona virus, bad people and bad governments may deliberately and strategically distribute debilitating or deadly microbes and even genetically manufacture viruses for different kind of warfare. Take the case of a group of lunatics or determined suicidal killers who infect themselves with a deadly virus of their own making and have a good lead time during which they can spread the disease before they

die. They will use subways, buses, supermarkets, and airplanes strategically to infect fellow humans by dispersing the virus via exhalation or infecting surfaces touched by other people, who will serve as involuntary collaborators during their incubation time. Deposits of deadly or debilitating viruses under government control in many countries are easily available for those governments and, to a lesser extent, for individuals. But known pathogens such as those for Ebola or other microbes can also be collected in their natural biotope, reproduced in larger quantities, and even modified for better use as weapons. – Humankind's global integration makes biological combat a weapon of choice for desperate killers who are either suicidal or intend to infect others who are willing or unwilling to be messengers of death. In our integrated, modern world, it will be difficult to keep the spread under control. Biological warfare might endanger those criminal states and politicians as well, except they can initiate strict border controls after the attack and/or store an antidote to protect their own population. Microbes manufactured for warfare or mass control in unruly societies need not be lethal, as long as they help dictators or aggressors make military forces or entire populations incapable of resistance for a limited time by causing serious disorientation, pain, or discomfort.

In naturally occurring pandemics, deadly pathogens are the enemy; in biological warfare, the human aggressors are the enemies and the pathogens their weapons of choice. The very few acute and preventive weapons for defense include: (1) complete, easy-to-understand public information and advice and (2) good public health infrastructures and pre-acute storage of remedies for easy distribution. Reducing freedom of mobility and other temporary restrictions in civil rights after the outbreak might become necessary as well. Official or voluntary quarantines in certain such as emergency offices, hospitals and nursing homes, and uninfected villages or provinces, as well as mandatory inoculations and other interventions are other extraordinary means necessary in winning the war. The goals of these extraordinary means need to be fully communicated before the outbreak. Preferably, independent, trusted individuals or groups of the civil society should simultaneously supervise such announcements. – When terrorists work alone in small cells, the best defense and prevention against all forms of terrorism and radical discontent in society is to support healthy cultural and ethical environments and to educate the populace to be risk competent and vigilant. Global high-tech networks of communication and travel allow good citizens as well as evildoers to work successfully in reaching their goals. Terrorists will most likely have direct or indirect support from one or more Mafia-type groups, even from governments and religious factions (like pirates had from official powers in the past). If this is the case, then those entities need to share the blame and punishment and must be exposed publicly. If biomedical killing of masses of innocent people is one of the options seriously contemplated by governments, the best defenses against this dangerous weapon are high levels of research and preparedness – and, unfortunately, a policy of threatening to retaliate similarly. During the Cold War, this approach was called the strategy of mutual assured destruction (MAD).

(2) Electric Risk and Electromagnetic Shock. Our sun emits various intensities of radiation constantly, from time to time it has been quite severe. In the past we did not care about it, however, and lacked the means to measure it. In September 1859, the biggest geomagnetic solar storm ever reported (called the Carrington Event after the British scientist who reported and documented it) destroyed many of the first telegraph lines in Europe and North America and caused a number of fires; a similar storm today would render the entire infrastructure of electricity and communication useless. Now we know, that extremely strong lengths and kinds of radiation will interfere with our electric networks and

may destroy hardware and software. But the same or similar radiation can also be initiated by states or by criminals using strong magnetic radiation as deliberate ammunition for destruction. If exploded in high air over Southern China or the East Coast of the United States (or fired from a harmless fishing trailer), a device similar to a hydrogen bomb that emits strong gamma radiation will render useless the digital infrastructure of the area encompassing Hong Kong, Shenzhen, and Guangdong or the Boston, New York, Philadelphia, Baltimore, Washington, D.C. corridor. The entire integrated electric grid will be affected, including microchips in phones, cars, supermarkets, and elevators, as well as all forms of digital communication and cooperation — including those of the police, military, rescue forces, and media. A 2008, U.S. Congress Commission on EMPs estimated that 90% of the U.S. population would die within 12 months after a total loss of electricity from starvation, disease, or societal breakdown (Pry 2013). People will die in their high-rise buildings and might kill each other over food and water. Cars will stop driving, and planes will fall out of the sky. People will be clueless as to what has caused the breakdown of civilization because the Internet and the media will not be functional. Attacks on utility infrastructures will have occurred and will likely occur again, destroying water dams, power grids, pumping stations, and all kinds of control systems. All sorts of private intellectual and real property will be stolen. The comfortable, civilized, highly complex, ultra-modern human bioculture elephant reveals that it is standing on feet of clay, and that it is literally built on sand, i.e. on silicon.

(3) Confidence Risk in Paper-and-Promise: Trade and commerce become more and integrated and thus are prey to unintentional or deliberate attacks on basic trust. The message 'in God we trust!' engraved on every US$ bill, becomes a genuine meaning. We had an unintentional meltdown of markets in real estate and finance in 2004 and 2008, and only concerted efforts to rescue those who had caused this meltdown avoided an international catastrophe in the bios of economy and business. Today, individual computer hackers or state-supported criminals can create total havoc in the fully integrated commercial life of the planet. Because high-frequency trading (HFT) is already done primarily by artificial intelligence, glitches or technical inequality in the software of trading machines and not human competence in trading will result in winning or losing. Hazardous legislation that is inept or corrupt still allows banks and other speculators to buy and manipulate commodities of all sorts; HFT has not proven to be economically necessary or beneficial; and governments print paper money uncontrolled. Un-

known or undisclosed leverage of market players, predatory lending, deregulation, and computer-driven interconnection and trading cause fragile business architectures of proportions as yet unknown (Wray 2012). We have speed limits on autobahns and streets for you and me, but there are no speed limits on trading commodities or derivate products for the 'big players.' Central banks and government market players distort markets by unpredictable currency moves creating 'trade anxiety'; currency trading maneuvers by big banks and governments reach US$5 trillion per day and make price predictions for manufacture and commerce impossible. Central banks also enjoy the liberty of printing as much 'promise on paper' money as they wish. Their most recent cynical strategy is to reduce the value of the paper money to initiate inflation and thus cause more inefficiencies in markets that have already been proven to be inefficient because of bubbles in real estate and stock market valuations created by those central banks. Most recent market manipulations have been done by central banks in a race to reduce their own currency against other currencies to make their products more attractive in world markets. One thing that will be achieved by such inefficient interventions into national and international markets is the reduction in value of government bonds and of paper money in pensions paid into by workers over their lifetimes. These governmental interventions and regulations have made the self-healing and adjusting market forces inefficient. They came into place after the gold standard was replaced by promise-on-paper bills only and certain other regulations guaranteed the survival of 'too big to fail' market players. On the other hand, reaction by other central banks in changing their own national interest rates results in developing market changes that will influence employment and profit, no matter what the other central bank expects from lowering or rising national interest rates and money supply. – I am not aware of tough, convincing proactive measures by states and businesses to avoid a global catastrophe that would render digital- or paper-based assets worthless.

Take this case: A crazy person, a group, or a government throws $800 billion in real U.S. Treasury bills on the European markets, not derivatives. The person request to be paid not in contracts or in futures, but to be paid and delivered immediately in scarce, real-value assets such as gold, silver, diamonds, land, corn, or cotton. Once those billions are offered, European markets will suffer a shock. Little trading occurs, and the markets shut down in no time. U.S. markets do not even open, nor do the Asian bourses. Scared people will run to their banks for paper money. Having no paper money anymore, my local bank closes the next day, and my neighborhood ATM machine is empty. Gas stations and supermarkets decline my credit cards, occasionally accepting promise-on-paper money or bartering goods or services. Because trust can easily be destroyed, even well-placed rumors for experts and the public might have already done the job of exposing the empty promises behind the signatures on paper money. Civil discontent towards promise-on-paper will lead to civil disobedience and disorder and result in sick political bodies.

(4) Revolt and Repression Risk: When Karl Marx searched in 1848 for huge human masses as a powerful force for changing unfair social and political environments, he identified the exploited proletarians of the early European industrial revolution. Today he would identify the unhappy and frustrated segments of populations in transition from traditional to modern societies. These include youth in the so-called Arab Spring and its counterrevolutions, global fashion modes of rebellion against traditions, and reactionary revolts against the fast-moving developments of global integration and the loss of traditional points of orientation in religion and culture. These losses have led to uncertainty and disorientation on the part of many young people, resulting in a rebirth of religious and cultural extremism and backward-oriented narrowness. Many studies have examined discontent in cultures and the changes, destruction,

and reconstruction brought about by rebellion Freud (Freud 2005) uses the psychoanalytical methods and principles to analyze social and cultural success and upheaval in cultures and countries just as he had earlier diagnosed diseases in individual persons. Most new centuries provides different reasons for confusion exploding into rebellion and discontent and many new forms of protest. At the same time, political dictators or strong social or business forces may use the same new communication and cooperation technologies for microscopic invasions of privacy, for indoctrination and introjection, or for promoting their own selfish interest in power. In his famous lectures on 'Biopower' at the College de France in 1978, Michel Foucault (1903) discussed the use of information and indoctrination methodology by nation states in Europe since the 18th century: 'when discipline is the technology deployed to make individuals behave, to be productive workers, biopolitics is deployed to manage population; for example to ensure a healthy workforce'. He traces the model of biopolitics back to the Greco-Roman and medieval emperors and kings; nowadays he might recognize the power of radio, television, and the Internet for even more successful forms of domination and indoctrination and their avoidance. A new 'political class', comparable to the feudal circles of yesterday and including networks of political officials and corporate leaders, conducts their own business, which is based on self-interest. New environments of information, communication, and cooperation based in cyberspace can work both ways, in favor of further liberation and the development of civil societies or in favor of state-controlled or business-controlled masses; in favor of better transparency or in favor of even more successful corruption and exploitation – similar to the double-purpose or spin-off use of old technology.

(5) Territorial Mix-Up Risk: In the old days, communities always had eremites, who left the 'real' world in order to emigrate into close communication and integration with non-geographical spiritual powers; they might, however, still been indirectly related to the 'real' world by praying for peace and divine intervention. Nowadays, emigrants from the 'real' world become famous citizens in 'Second Life' or other internet territories as celebrated orchestra conductors or famous singers, football and boxing stars, inventors and savers of humankind, while at the same time they are 'nobodies' living unknown and not socially integrated or even recognized in their private quarters. 'This is not a game, this is the real life' is widely quoted slogan of one of the internet portals. Internet addiction has become one of the most difficult disorders to treat in psychiatric therapy.

(6) Loss of Control Risk: Much is talked about, particularly in science fiction narratives, the threat from artificial intelligence, turning against the existing balance of interaction and interdependence among the wide modern world of bios. Not much is known yet precisely about systems of mad and aggressive artificial intelligence turning outside of their sphere, running rampage in taking control of local or global automation, destroying all or some integrated forms of in the world of modern human bios, such as mad and aggressive individuals today cause destruction by killing fellow humans with traditional explosives or deadly infectious microbes (Diamond 2006).

Well-functioning digital and microbial infrastructures and more or less harmonious biological, economic, social and political bodies are essential for the survival of the bios of our modern culture, but they have made the new complex adaptable and integrated of collective and political bios more vulnerable in many new dimensions. All in all, these six scenarios demonstrate the not yet widely enough discussed risk of the impressive colossus of the modern global and integrated political body with its vulnerable cultural and economic organs.

6

Cultures and Modifications in the Body of the Leviathan

Political and corporate bodies are of similar living material as individual bodies, but they are not identical, in the words of Confucius '*similar but not identical.*' The same can be said for societies and states of humans as for biotopes of microbes, states of bees and ants, natural and cultivated environments, and the myriads of microbiomes. Biotopes and individual bios are in permanent transition from one point in life to the next, changing themselves and changing their sceneries as well. Transition and interacting adaptation is part of life and the rule of life. Those rules are similar for the body politic as for bodies of individual people. The front cover engraving on Hobbes (1651) 'Leviathan or the Matter, Former and Power of a Common Wealth Ecclesiastical and Civil' by Abraham Bosse presents a human body consisting of a multitude of skin cells showing diverse individual citizens, surmounted by a royal person, holding a sword and a spiritual stick as symbols of united physical and spiritual powers; the title is surrounded by images of a castle, a tank, a farming landscape, a house, a meeting place and other symbols of the political bios. Internal metabolism of all organs and good interaction with other body politics depends on internal and external communication and cooperation. Competence in managing internal and external affair and internal competition and competition with other societies and states keeps the body politics fit and strong. Calculating adequately the best way to keep the body healthy and from time to time contemplating and reviewing internal and external risks and affairs promotes harmony and cultivates political bodies together with their surrounding political territories. The 'integrating matter' may be a king or emperor or head of state or, in Confucian reasoning the 'son of heaven', or even a spiritual continuity 'by God's grace' within or outside of the blood-line of the actual head of state and representing wholeness and continuity of the political body.

An old Taoist (Laozi: 57) wisdom 2000 years earlier, informs the Leviathan about essentials of successful leadership in healthy and strong political bodies: 'Rule the land with justice, fight a war with surprise, and win a country with harmonious action (wuwei). How do I know that this? The more prohibitions we have, the more rebellious the people will be. The sharper the weapons are under the people, the more turbulent the land will be. The shrewder the people, the more abnormal things occur. The more

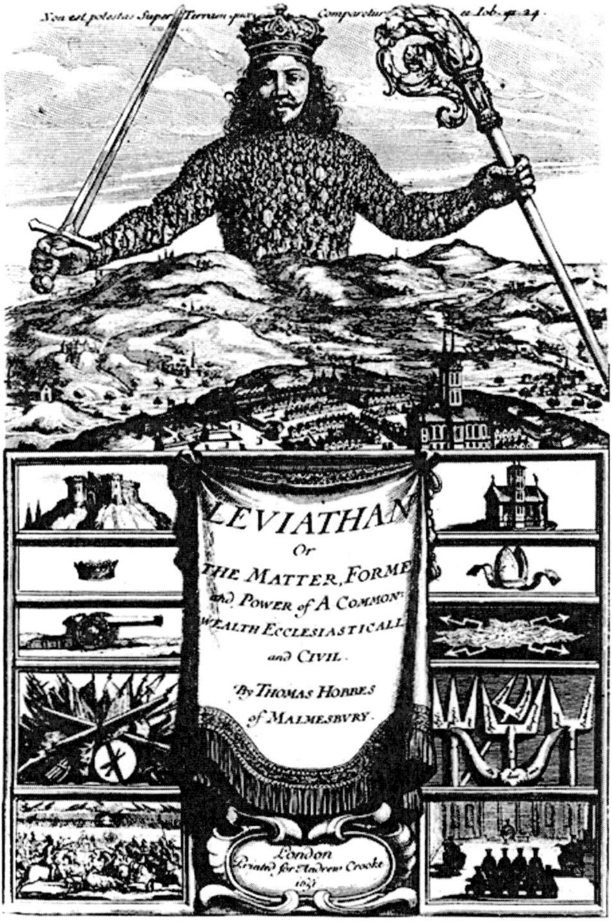

laws there are, the more thieves and robbers will be there. Therefore, the wise person says: When I am not greedy, the people will become rich by themselves.

When I act with harmony, the people will change by themselves. When I refrain from imposing, the people will do justice by themselves. When I refrain from craving, the people will get rid of their cravings'.

Modern societies are symbiotic, complex and adoptable living beings of natural persons, natural communities such as families, clans and villages or neighborhoods, and economic and legal persons such as enterprises, institutions, bureaucracies, and similar cyberspace based persons, communities, and powers. They all want to live well, to grow, and to sustain their lives and networks; this might lead to cooperation and support, network building, favoritism, mutual aid and help, also to corruption and exploitation in the interest of survival and protecting and even expanding one's biotope and influence. These tendencies of different players can and do lead to dysfunctional bodies and biotopes (Fukuyama 2014). Haidt (2012) argues that our individual feelings and instincts to belong and to be connected form our personalities stronger than our rationality; he calls for 'reflection and reform' to 'understand and overcome' those religious and political instincts, which intertwine our natural social instincts to belong with others. Bees live in complex and highly structured social and biological communities, but sometimes they suddenly abandon their hives, a phenomenon described as 'colony collapse disorder' (Lu et al. 2014). We humans on and off destroy our complex political, cultural, social and economic communities as we see these days in some Arab and Muslim countries, a phenomenon for which we may describe as 'culture collapse disorder', based on discontent, hate, extreme ideology, terror, exploitation, and just widespread unhappiness and the loss of mutual trust and mutual aid. In the coming age of globalization and the internet, national or regional states are going to share their integrating power and matter with other social, cultural, communal, and political bodies; loyalties of citizens might be divided in more complicated way than just between churches and nation states.

Individual bodies might be more integrated than political ones; but political bodies may come in more shapes and shades than individual bodies. Some body parts such as Mafiosi, dictators, and leaders of good or bad dominating economic, religious or social groups might be happy and healthy while the rest of the political and social body suffers and is sick because of negligence or exploitation. Political bodies strive on the same 8 C biological properties; they need internal and external communication and cooperation as their blood stream and nervous system, competence and competition in survival, contemplation and calculation in order to set their vision and goal into practice, compassion in dealing with their constituency, and good skills in cultivation for extending their live into the future. – We also find the 3 F's – *foods, funs, faiths* – as good constituents for long and happy lives of political bodies. *Food* in form of foodstuffs, other materials for individual and collective living such as housing, police, military, and hospitals is the basis for living together. *Fun* and satisfaction is essential for harmony and happiness of the various cells and parts of the political body; it includes festivals, good entertainment, and good housing, symphony orchestras and libraries, radio and television, enjoyment in having friends and families and making babies. *Faith* may be religious faith, but in a wider sense faith and trust in solidarity and camaraderie, in equal or relatively equal civil and human rights, in the sustainability and even improvement of existing social, political and cultivated biotopes, of course for some also faith in a higher order of harmony created and promised by Gods, a spiritual togetherness and brotherhood in human bios and culture.

7

Constructing Healthy Modular Public Bodies

Public things and beings, in comparison to individual and private things and beings, have been called 'res publica'. The term republic has the same roots, but other political bodies are called kingdom, empire, democracy, aristocracy. Similar to individual bodies and other forms of bios, one size does not fit all. Aristotle already had described different bodies of political bios and their advantages and disadvantages, suggesting a harmonious blend of meritocracy and individual virtue. Oligarchic and democratic bodies can deteriorate into totalitarian and anarchic bios, but neither power nor commerce is the life purpose of the body politic, rather happiness and body healthy. Healthy families and clans are the biological matter in forming healthy, strong and happy political bodies; this comes close to the Confucian model of the state being one large family in the wide world of bios consisting out of smaller families. Hobbes, in assuming that people naturally are egoistic and self-centered – 'homo homini lupus', one human is the other's wolf –, called for a strong powerful state to prevent killings and wars and to enforce harmony. Spinoza (1670) had a more complex understanding of the bios politic as a highly adaptable complex form of life and argued that, because of us humans being endowed with our spirit by God, freedom and peace, should not harm the body politic, because the elimination of freedom and peace would as well eliminate the state. Coming from a Jewish family who was prosecuted in Portugal, he argued in his 'Theological-political Tractatus', that 'the freedom to philosophize can be granted without threatening piety and peace, and that on the contrary the elimination of freedom and piety will threaten the state itself'.

Long lasting states and societies seem to have a rather modular body of more or less loosely integrated or interacting parts which allowed for transformations and modifications once one or the other part became weak, distressed, sclerotic, cancerous, or otherwise threatening the others or the entire body. Vast political bodies with relatively long lives were not run on a short dominant leash. The vast empire of the Mongolian Emperor Genghis Khan in the 13th century was a supercenter over multiple more or less independent political bodies enjoying certain freedoms of religion and internal affairs. Charlemagne run his European empire with only a few hundred people at the center, among them a few dozen riding messengers carrying mail to his various relatively independent fortresses.

The more successful emperors of China ruled the provinces and instructed the mandarins by royal letters and only in most dangerous situations had to seek solutions and protect the body politics by war. The multi-centered 1000 years of the Holy Roman Empire were marked by various interacting power bodies of kings, princes, dukes, bishops, and free cities in a decentralized manner, also by relatively autonomous rural peasant communes owning most lands and having their own rules and traditions on how to work the lands together as a commune or allocate of certain families. None of these political bodies were nation states, similar to those which have developed over the last 200 years.

New cyber-territories allow the individual to escape from a local neighborhood in which she or he does not feel to be integrated or does not want to be active part of. Such conditions would not make a strong and stable local community on which the lager body politic can rest. Of course, individuals will not and should not become indistinguishable from their local neighborhood as this also would weaken the local community because good modular and adaptive forces within houses and neighborhoods would be missing and thus reduce the health and flexibility of the neighborhood bios. Good interaction with geographical and cyberspace territories will only strengthen the survivability of those new neighborhoods and high-rises and mega-cities by making them fit to adapt flexibly to new modifications of the ever changing body politic.

Czar Nikolas I in 1852 used biomedical terminology to describe the weakening Ottoman Empire as 'the sick man at the Bosporus'. After 1000 years of good health and periods of great cultural and political success the empire had lost the vigor of life by arthritis and sclerosis of the body and by infections from the outside such as from the colonial powers of France and Britain. Dormant rivalries between Shiite and Sunnite denominations together with new tribal conflicts using extreme interpretations of Muslim traditions have and still mark the demise of a formerly great body politic. US American meddling and military and political intervention devoid of any understanding of prevailing basic cultures of personal and tribal loyalty added to further metabolic and anxiety disorders of the successor bodies, so do geopolitical squabbles about influence peddling around the destructed or already cadaveric remains. Metastasizing cancerous diseases in the families of sick political offsprings of the former Ottoman Empire extend into Europe, challenged by anxiety disorder caused by too many refugees not familiar with traditional body functioning in pluralistic Western societies and themselves being within walls of despair and fear. Old social and political bodies such as Iraq and Syria are disintegrating, infected by some sort of 'cancer' or 'auto-immune disorder'. Societies unwilling or incapable to modify into the modern world have been called 'sclerotic'; there are other coronary or infectious diseases, dementia, hypertension, diabetes, arteriosclerosis in many modern societies and cultures, in businesses, corporations and communities, some related to the rapidly changing half-time of social change. But there is also 'preventive health care' for political bodies: democratic fitness training and body building, and the support of happiness in the cultural and social biotopes of economy and politics, in clans, communities, healthy and growing countries and weak and disintegrating societies.

In which biological terms should we describe the various biopolitical stages of good or mediocre health, of various diseases or disorders in the Chinese political body from the times of the Yellow Emperor to the demise of the Manchu Dynasty 100 years ago, after the Boxer Rebellion, corruption, hypocrisy, ignorance, other societal diseases in combination with sickening infections and invaders coming from the outside, reformulating the role of the 'son of heaven' by Mao and various ways by his successors and the Chinese people? Was the Cultural Revolution a necessary and healthy body cleaning or another disorder in a body politic in transition to find back to his old or to newer forms of health for such a large body? Did the Leninist revolution in Russia follow the blueprint of Marx 1848 Communist Manifesto or was it a more complex and painful way to transform Mother Russia and later the larger Soviet Bloc, which included a quite diverse group of political bodies, in the modern age? Marx did not expect that Russia would ever have a proletarian revolution, because it was lacking large numbers of exploited proletarians in comparison to Germany and England (Sass 2003).

Yesterday the bios of culture was threatened by foreign invaders, corrupt officials, individual bad people in my community or even family; today and even more tomorrow the bios of culture and community can be threatened by individuals and groups from far away destroying cyberspace environments of our geographic cultures and lives. We see a new 'localism' (Moore 2014, Schuhmacher 1973) as a form of geographical patriotism in a complex adaptation and modification based on discontent in our cultural and political bios or will powerful adaptive body politics eat up and integrate these newly developed alternative nerve systems into their body? 'Whole Community Recovery', a project by the Royal Society of Arts in London (Pascoe, Robson 2105), explores the role of social networks, connected communities, sustainability and whole person happiness and satisfaction in biopolitical perspective for similar communities in deterioration and people in discontent despite already established special services for the addicted, the poor and the sick. Future decentralization tendencies and movements will a positive contribution towards sustaining or even regaining community and geographic modularity which has demonstrated to be a central property in the survival of complex adaptive systems. Highly centralized and not very modular political bodies have less opportunities to recognize and implement health and happiness supporting initiatives from one of their organs or from grass-root levels and thus are threatened to sudden political failure and losing the sparks of individual and communal creativity, competition and innovation for modifying their body bios and its living body parts. New localism might or might not be multicultural; it would be stronger and healthier if it would allow for cultural and social modularity.

It is only natural that the enormously expanding bios of integrated geography and cyberspace overwhelms many individuals and communities as information overflow and confusing new options for flexible adaption into new territories are too powerful. Reduction of complexity then is one of the strategies to cope with new information and options by protecting or regaining individual identity and self-respect by finding integration in hopefully harmonious and less confusing healthier interactive biotopes which offer solidarity and camaraderie, friendship and a new personal identity in such groups or movements in new and simple territories of local geography and supportive and attractive cyberspace. But such a reduction of complexity and modularity can become dangerous for the life of the 'corps politie' and 'corps sociale' and does not seem to be the healthiest way of cultivating self-identity within the larger social and political body. At the end of a confrontational with Job (Job 40f), God boasts about his powers in creating all forms of bios on land and in the sea, the most powerful of them the gigantic land creature Behemoth and the most powerful sea dragon Leviathan: 'Behold, Behemoth which I made as I made you, he eats grass like an ox,... he is the first of the works of God, ... can you draw out Leviathan with a fishhook... upon earth there is not his like, a creature without ease; he beholds everything that is high; he is king over all the sons of pride'.

The mythological animals of Behemoth and Leviathan had played a role already in the mythology of the Sumer dynasties, 7000 years ago in Mesopotamia around Ur. The Gross Happiness Product of the future might have to be delivered by often bellicose, and rarely harmonious, interaction between these two powers. Euphrates and Tigris in Assyria, the Yangtzekiang in China, the Danube and Rhine in Europe, the Volga in Russia, and the Mississippi in North America were the travel routes for material goods and for religions, philosophies and knowledge; the Mediterranean became the 'inland' water body for Phoenician, Greek, and Roman cultures. Then oceanic shipping routes were developed and railroads and autobahns formed wider and more stable networks of commerce and ideas. Now, it is the interplay between the geographic Behemoth giants and the cyberspace Leviathan dragons, which will decide the future of human civilization and culture. 300 years ago in 1716 the Ottoman Empire attacked the Christian Habsburg Empire, but was defeated by famous Price Eugen. Today in 2014 young German boys and girls in remote villages of Westphalian provinces in Germany learn about Islam, become fanatic, travel in t-shirt and with backpack to Muslim countries in the Middle East and behead Muslims. The first battle in 1716 was the fight between two Behemoths on land, the battle of today is the battle of the Leviathan against the Behemoths on land and in cyberspace. On September 11, 2001, the widely unknown little Leviathan Al Kaida attacked the most powerful Behemoth at the World Trade Center, and the USA Behemoth declared war against this ever growing Leviathan. Events in Syria, Irak and Libya over the last years have also Leviathanian feedbacks in European cities such as

Hamburg, Paris and London, where Muslim Kurds and fanatic Sunnite Muslims fight each other in the streets of the European Behemoth countries, of which they are a part. Recently the liquid water dragon has conquered lands in Syria and Iraq and given birth to a new Behemoth of a radical Muslim Caliphate and exercised dominance on lands and people. Behemoth and Leviathan interact with each other. Our dreams are of Leviathanian nature but they need to be embodied in the lands of the Behemoth for realized and lived happiness of people and communities. Are individual human bodies and cultural and political bodies really different when they are aspiring joy and happiness and end up in cancer and despair?

Hobbes gave the body politic which was taming, dominating, and punishing, the name of the sea dragon Leviathan; he meant the geographic organization of robust human society. Today we may recognize the interacting and fighting powers of the land giant and the sea dragon symbolized in the powers of lands in cities, streets, police and military forces, factories and businesses, and the powers of the sea dragon in the fluidity of dreams and visions and the realities of internets of peoples and things, grapping more and more powers from the lands into the interconnected waters, streams, and lands as the new ecosystems. Many images display the struggle between the two beasts, symbolizing not only for us humans the eternal struggle for life and struggle in life, the 'elan vital' for all forms of bios, but also and in particular for the human bios. For us humans, the Behemoth represents the strong lands and fortified cities, the armies of soldiers and military might; the Leviathan lived in the running streams and water bodies and nowadays in the liquid powers of the all invasive internet. According to Jewish and Christian traditions, God at the 'day of reckoning' end the 'struggle of life' and kill the demonic serpentines (Apocalypse 20:2ff); Hinduism and Buddhism have similar narrative addressing the end of life's struggles.

Lao Zi once said: 'Cultivate the self and virtue will be true; cultivate the family and virtue will be complete; cultivate the village and virtue will grow; cultivate the country and virtue will be rich; cultivate the world and virtue will be wide.' (Dao te Ching 54). We can expand and translate Lao Zi's insight into a Bioethical Imperative for the 21st Century: 'Cultivate yourself and life and virtue becomes true; cultivate individual and corporate persons and virtue will be great; cultivate political and corporate bodies and virtue will be full; cultivate communication and cooperation and life will grow; cultivate compassion and competence and life will be rich; cultivate the worlds of bios and virtues will be wide.' In regard to building corporations and institutions as well-respected, rich, and successful corporate persons practicing bioethics anywhere and everywhere in the world, we may say: Cultivate communication and cooperation and corporate persons and communities will be strong; cultivate competence and compassion and corporate persons and communities will be good; cultivate corporate persons and communities and the neighborhood will be healthy; cultivate the neighborhoods and the world will be healthy and happy.

The 21st century has already demonstrated that it will most likely see even more strength and power in the reign of the Leviathan via new fluidity in the globalization of all forms of bios and in the digital waters of the Internets of people and of things. Inhabitants of Facebook have outnumbered the inhabitants of China since 2014; social networks vastly enlarge my options to meet people and make friends beyond my geographical village. Global emailing, blogging, and digital files outstrip the role of handwritten letters and printed books for communication and cooperation in science, culture, and information. Microbial bios, infections, and potential warfare travel by airwaves rather than traditional waterways. Old and new religious and spiritual traditions populate the minds of individuals and form fluid, non-geographical living communities and cultures, both small and large. Internet-based production and commerce compete with local markets of work, trade, and vision. Traditional armies, navies, and air forces are supplemented by electromagnetic guns and mortars or by biological warfare. Unparalleled destructive powers hide unseen in the darkness of Leviathanian nuclear submarine 'dragons' that attack underwater. Age-old ideologies, which might have been useful in protecting the lifestyles and territories of nomadic tribes in remote lands infiltrate unhappy people around the globe who search for guidance in the unchartered waters of oversupply in information, orientation, and guidance. The liquid powers of the Leviathan inflame the neural networks of individuals and communities and threaten the biological stability of the Behemoth in local governments and global cultures, in intolerant and tolerant communities alike. Cultures, communities, and individuals need to redefine their roles in the struggle between the Behemoth and the Leviathan in shorter and shorter half-lives of adjustment and alteration.

Lao Tzu (Dao te Ching 11), in discussing spatial and geographic rooms and human bios, said; 'We build Rooms with Windows and Doors, but it is the Inner Space which makes the Room livable'. Indeed, we build our own rooms: living rooms and sleeping rooms, hotel rooms and hospital rooms, operating rooms and hospice rooms, concert halls and town halls, factory halls and dancing halls, torture chambers and court chambers, office rooms and

chatrooms, – what happens in these rooms depends on me and you. Also, these rooms themselves may not last forever and are threatened by arsonists, shortenings in cables of electricity or communication, by breaking doors and windows, by stealing values, by spreading rumors, by poisoning rooms in many other ways. Humankind has, just alike a tree and all other bios, only this one geospace and we may destroy it technologically or lose it by cyberspace migration and relocation instead of enjoying and promoting good and stable complex adaptable integrations and interactions in cultivating health and happiness of individual and collective bodies, just like a good old tree with strong roots and successful photosynthesis.

What can/should we do? Did John Lennon had a valuable bio-philosophical insight: 'We've got this gift of love, but love is like a precious plant. You can't just accept it and have it in the cupboard or just think it's going to get on by itself. You have to keep watering it. You're got to really look after it and nurture it'.

Reflecting and mediating the interactive and integrated ecosystems and interactive networks in biology, society, business, technology and communication, we may – in reference to Pastor Fritz Jahr's 'Bio-Ethical Imperative: Respect every living being as an end in itself and treat it, if possible, as such' – discuss a wider integrated ecological, corporate and political 'Bio-Cultural Imperative: Respect and support direct human inter-action and common-sense as an end in itself and use hardware and software tools only in stabilizing healthy and happy cultures in the bodies of ecologies, corporations and politics'.

8

A CONCLUDING NARRATIVE: THE LITTLE TOWN BY THE RIVER

I have used the following narrative about 'The Little Town by the River' (Sass 2016:53-56) in classroom teachings and conferences on various continents to encourage discussion about tolerance and working-together in happy and healthy diversified political bodies and urban biotopes. The story is influenced by the Prophet Mohamed's 'Contract of Medina' (Hamidullah 1975), which he devised in 46 paragraphs, after his escape from Mecca to Medina, supporting harmony and tolerance, and cultural and economic success in a complex multicultural society.

THE LITTLE TOWN BY THE RIVER: This town is really small, measured by the long river and the surrounding hills small like a drop at a bucket. But it happens to be the only town beside the river and the people are proud of their town, the river stream and their great wealth. This wealth they see in the dignity and nobleness of their citizens, their different city quarters and their cultivated lands and waters. Freedom and security of the citizens is cherished above all. They help each other and lend a hand to the young generation to act responsively, to respect 'others', even if they do not share the opinions or their absolute values. They loathe lies, theft, killing, injustice, egotism, arrogance, and intolerance. To lie, to steal and to murder will be punished even when thieves and murders pretend to act in the name of God or out of a higher insight. They do not all believe in God; yet they all are of the opinion that, if there were a God, he would forbid to kill, to steal and to lie. This is also expressed by those living in Jewish, Christian and Moslem houses and streets of the 'Almighty and Merciful'. They who believe in God are also aware of the power of Satan; all know of the evil in Man and about evil persons they feel obliged to fight against. They detest intolerance and spare no effort to create a culture of communication and cooperation by listening and arguing based on trust.

Each of them has a special competence and competes with others in improving and protecting the common goods of their integrated city bios. Of course, they are free to contemplate about bios, biotopes, and creation in their own individual fashion, with or without networks of friends, and to draw conclusions from their insights and intuitions in calculating their own position and the improvement of their service and integration within their town. Respect for each other and the entire world of bios surrounding them and compassion with each other, in particular with the weak, the desperate, the sick and needy is the basis of their harmony and their richness in valuables and values. Communication and cooperation, competence and competition, contemplation and calculation, compassion and cultivation are the pillars on which their individual and collective culture is based and they all are aware that these 8 C's needs to be protected and defended against evildoers from the inside and aggressors from the outside.

It is their opinion that human dignity finds expression mainly in respecting the dignity of the individual conscience. They honor the position of each fellow citizen in respect to their final religious or philosophical conviction as inviolable. Overall, they respect and request the individual's conscience responsibility; they don't accuse each other of immorality or being uncultured when their own judgment in matters of moral and culture differ from others. Even if they cannot accept the conviction of their fellow-citizens or regard those to be abstruse, they will do everything that these fellow-humans will not be forced to do and act against their conviction and conscience. For example, foods are labeled as to signify whether they are kosher, vegetarian or organically grown. Nobody is forced to take medication or abort unborn life, to donate or accept organs or to take on work that violates personal values and religious or humanist beliefs. Whenever someone proposes to put pressure on the conscience of others, they all turn very angry because thereby they see a violation of the dignity of the little town and the wealth of values of their citizens and communities. Most city laws contain a 'sunset clause' that indicates that a law will use its force after a specific number of years, unless it has been extended or modified; they also include a 'conscience clause', that allows citizens to request exemption on the grounds of conscience as long as this is possible without bringing harm to others.

The citizens of this town live in harmony with their natural biotopes and the many other forms of bios, which they have cultivated with microbes, plants, animals, colonies, and which they respect as 'brothers and sisters' within and around the bios of their city. They take great pride in having their own healthy personal microbiome and in creating probiotic biotopes in their houses, schools, offices, factories, assembly halls, parks and agricultures. They enjoy reaching out to other people and cities, making prudent use of their 8 C properties all the way around the globe by the water ways of their stream, by roads and airways, by digital networks of commerce and manufacturing, by communication and cooperation in social networks, by finding friends and partners, cultivating friendships and partnerships just as they do in their geographical locality.

A look at the architecture of the houses provides a clear view of the cultural and ethical structure of this city at the water. As different as they appear, these houses are built on the 8 C pillars in the basement and the first floors, which are connected for the purpose of security of the inhabitants and the city as a whole against hunger, murder, torture, and for the care and sake of all who cannot help themselves. However, the layout and the furnishing in the upper floors indicate show the rich variety in values and visions of their owners and inhabitants. There are debates in one of the houses whether or not a human fetus has a personal moral or legal right or is to be seen a part of the body of the mother and the personal dignity of the pregnant person. In another house we hear debates whether religious rules for fasting may be broken in case of illness in order to give medicine and nutrition to patients. The century-old debate about the question whether a terminally ill hoping for life after death should ask for the 'poisoned drink' currently has been toned down; but there are adamant calls that physicians make better use of palliative medicine in easing pain and suffering and thus making euthanasia discussions and ensuing abuse unnecessary. On the rooftops, we hear the loudest and most exhaustive and sometimes crazy debates, arguing those very complex questions whether God is one person in three or three in one or a person at all, whether there is one main prophet or even a representative of God on earth, whether all things in nature are divine and require adequate respect or not, whether there are invisible spirits or demons and whether they have power over us or the world of bios. Furthermore, whether human zygotes ensouled and may be resurrected in paradise or take part in the process of reincarnation? Do individual souls transmigrate, do animals or plants have souls, do transgenic animals having human DNA therefore also have a part of a human soul or spirit? Does one have to believe in a higher spiritual authority in order to be a decent person and a good fellow-citizen?

Debates like these have gone on for a long time and most likely will never stop. In their own way these quarrels represent the great richness of values and visions of this little town by the river. In some of the houses, people are sympathetic to such eccentric palaver, others are not and sometimes judge it as silly, absurd, and not necessary for being a valued member of the city community. Some are of the opinion that these are things that are 'divine secrets' and as such call for modesty rather than righteousness. Nevertheless, everyone would go out of the way to secure the right of convincing, discourse, quarrel, and dissent to the disputing parties. There is an awareness and appreciation that reasoning in the upper floors do influence the deeds on the lower ones and rightly so, as long as fellow humans are respected and supported and not hurt or belittled. But they do not accept when individuals or clans violate the rules of civility in the community. Whoever does not like those local rules and ways of life will be free to move somewhere else, and it goes without saying that as long as people live in the village as citizens or guests, they have to respect these rules of mutual respect and the dignity of their fellow humans.

The names of the streets and plazas remind the citizens of their common history and the roots of the town's culture. One of the squares is dedicated to the victims of murder, violence, and terrorism, to the slain burned residents of Jericho and Ai, Nanjing and Dresden, the victims of innumerable pogroms of Jews, of the tortured and burned of the so-called Holy Inquisition, of the rape of Nanjing, and the victims of global terrorism such as at the World Trade Center in New York City. Houses of Contemplation have murals representing the integrated and integrating harmony of the bios of the city and its surroundings.

REFERENCES

Al-Farabi 2001 Selected Aphorisms, NY Cornell U.

Aristotle, Politeia.

Asimov I 1942 ('Runabout' 1942), Handbook of Robotics 2058!, 56. edition.

Bhutan 2013 GNH 11th Five-Year Plan Self-reliance and inclusive green socioeconomic Development, vol. 2, Bhutan.

Cox-Foster DL, Conlan S, Holmes EC et al 2007 A metagenomic Survey of Microbes in Honey B Colony Collapse Disorder, in: Science 312 (5848) 383-287.

De Pizan C 1407 Livre de Corps Politic.

Diamond J 2006 Collapse. How Societies choose to Fail or Succeed. New York: Viking.

Fan R 2016 Non-egalitarian social Responsibilities for Health, in: Kennedy Inst of Ethics J 26(2) 204.

Foucault M 1903 Society must be defended, pp. 239-264.

Freud S 2005 Civilization and Its Discontents (Unbehagen in der Kultur, 1930).

Fukuyama F 2014 The Sources of Political Dysfunktion, in: Foreign Affairs Sept/Oct 2014: 5-26.

Hamidullah M 1975 The first written Constitution in the World, Lahore: Askrat Press 1975.

Haidt J 2012 Why good People are divided by Politics and Religion, NY Random House.

Hegel, Vorlesungen zur Geschichte der Philosophie, Jubilaeumsausgabe, Bd. 11: 63, cf also 11: 45f, 151ff.

Hershock PD 2012 Buddhist Reflections of Realizing a more equitable global Future, NY: Sunny.
Hillis D 2019 The first Machine Intelligences, in Possible Minds, ed. J Brockman, NY Penguin Press 2019, 171-177.
Hobbes T 1651 Leviathan or the Matter, Former and Power of Common Wealth Ecclesiasical and Civil. Hamburg.
Jahr F 2013 Essay in Bioethics 1924-1948, Zuerich: LIT.
Langdon Forham F 2002 The political Theory of Christine de Pizan, Burlington VT.
Lu C, Warchol KM, Callahan KA 2014 Sub-lethal exposure to neonicotinoids impaired honey bees winterization before proceeding to colony collapse disorder, in: Bulletin of Insectology 67(1) 125-130.
Kishore RR 2017 in: 1926-2016 Fitz Jahr's Bioethics. A global Discourse, rd. A Muzur, HM Sass, Zuerich: Lit, p. 94.
Kline L 2017 Inside the World of Teledildonics, where Sex Toys meet Social Media, in: Rooster Magazine, Boulder 10-31-2017.
Mancuso ST 2018 The revolutionary Genius of Plants, NY: Simon & Schuster.
Mendelsohn M 1819 Jerusalem oder über religiöse Macht und Judentum, Ofen: Burian, p. 201.
Moellering G 2006 Reason, Routine, Reflexology, Oxford 4. ed: Elsevier.
Money NP 2014 The Amoeba in the Room. Lives of the Microbes. Oxford U Press.
Moore MM 2014 (5th ed) Localism. A Philosophy of Government. Ridge Enterprise Publ.

Newman WR 2006 Atoms and Alchemy, U Chicago Press.
Pascoe S, Robson J (Royal Society of Arts, Action and Research Center) 2015 Whole Community Recovery. The Value of People, Place and Community. London.
Pry PV 2013 Electric Armageddon, in: CreateSpace; Metatech Corporation for Oak Ridge National Laboratory, January 2010 'Report Meta-R-320'.
Reeves M, Levin S, Ueda D 2016 The Biology of Corporate Survival, in: Harvard Business Review, p. 49.
Sahlberg P, Doyle W 2019 Let the Children play: How Play save our Schools and help Children thrive, NY Oxford U Pres.
Sass HM 1983 The Transition from Feuerbach to Marx, in: Studies in Soviet Thought 26: 123-142.
Sass HM 2003 Common Moral Principles and Cultural Diversity, in: Formosan J Medical Humanities (4).
Sass HM 2006 Bioethics and Biopolitcs. Beijing Lectures by a European Scholar. [Chinese / English edition] Xian: 4th Military Medical Univ Press; press.fmmu.
Sass HM 2009 Ethische Risiken und Prioritäten bei Pandemien. Bochum: ZME.
Sass HM 2012 Ludwig Feuerbach über virtuelle Realität im Internet, in: Aufklärung und Kritik 19(2): 29-37.
Sass HM 2014 An Early Hegelian Vision of the Internet. Ernst Kapp's 1845 Philosophy of Cultivating Space and Time, in: Jahrb für Hegelforschung. St Augustin: Academia, 15/17: 11-34.
Sass HM 2014 What is Bios and how to protect and promote its Cultivation?, in: Proceedings of the International Symposium on Bioculturology. Guangdong Life

Culture Association and Guangdong Medical College, Dongguan 2014: 1-12.
Sass HM 2016 Cultures in Bioethics Zuerich: LIT.
Sass HM 2018 Bioethics and Biopolitics in Cultivating Bios an Biotopes, in: Darulfunun Ilahiyat, Istanbul U 29 (2): 167-179.
Sass HM 2019 Homo Faber. The Impact of Tool Use Cultures on Ecosystems and Society, in: J Artificial Intelligence Humanities, 4: 9-30.
Schuhmacher EF 1973 Small is Beautiful. Economics as if People Matter. NY: Harper.
Smith R, Barry R 2019 Russian Hack exposes weakness in US Power Grid, in: Wall Street J Jan 11, 2019 p A1, A9.
Spinoza B 1670 Tractatus Theologico-Politicus contingens dissertationes aliquot, quibus ostenditur Libertatem philosophandi non tantum falva Pietate and Reipublicae Pace posse concendi; sed candem nisi com Pace Reipublicae, ipsaque Pietate tolli non posse. Hamburg.
Vasquez I, Porcnik T 2018 The Human Freedom Index HFI. A global Measurement of Personal, Civil and Economic Freedom, Wash DC: Cato.
Wilson EO 1975 Sociobiology, Harvard U Press.
Wilson DH 2012 Robocalype. New York: Vintage Books.
Woolsey RJ, Pry PV 2014 The Growing Threat from an EMP Attack, in: Wall Street Week, August 13: A13.
Wray LR 2012 Modern Money Theory. Palgrave Macmillan.
Zhai XM 2011 Diversified and in Harmony, but not Identical, in: Asian Bioethics Review 3: 31-35.

Zhong N 2014 The Concept of Family Happiness of Chinese People. A perspective of Bioculturoly, in: Proceedings of the International Symposium on Biocultur-ology, Guodong Life Culture Association, 152-159.

HANS-MARTIN SASS

Hans-Martin Sass was born 1935 in Hagen, Westfalen, and now lives in Reston, Virginia. He holds faculty positions in philosophy and bioethics at Ruhr University, Bochum, FRG (since 1966), and Georgetown University, Washington DC (since 1980); he is also Honorary Professor at Renmin University (1985) and Peking Union Medical College (2001) in Beijing PRC. In 2015, the Federal Republic of Germany conferred the Officers's Cross of Merit (Bundesverdienstkreuz) on Professor Sass. His Curriculum Vitae includes 100+ separate publications, 250+ journal articles, 300+ invited lectures.

Politica et Ars

Interdisziplinäre Studien zur politischen Ideen- und Kulturgeschichte
hrsg. von Prof. Dr. Richard Saage, Prof. Dr. Walter Reese-Schäfer und Prof. Dr. Eva-Maria Seng

Richard Saage
Otto Bauer
Ein Grenzgänger zwischen Reform und Revolution
Bd. 28, 2020, ca. 256 S., ca. 39,90 €, br., ISBN 978-3-643-14625-0

Hans Ulrich Seeber
Globalisierung, Utopie und Literatur
Von Thomas Morus (1516) bis Darcy Ribeiro (1982)
Globalisierung und Utopie sind eng aufeinander bezogen. Erstens setzte die Entstehung der literarischen Utopie im Zeitalter der Entdeckungen (More, *Utopia*, 1516) eine globale Ausweitung der Perspektive voraus, welche die soziale Phantasie beflügelte und erlaubte, den Vorstellungen einer idealen Gesellschaft einen plausiblen geographischen Ort zuzuweisen. Zweitens wurden die Entwürfe mit der Entfesselung der Globalisierung einerseits naturbezogener (pastorale Utopie), andererseits immer globaler, ja planetarischer. Sie führte zur Vision einer neuen Weltordnung, zuerst in Wells' *A Modern Utopia* (1905).
Bd. 27, 2017, 266 S., 34,90 €, br., ISBN 978-3-643-13618-3

Richard Saage
Auf den Spuren Utopias
Stationen des utopischen Denkens von der Frühen Neuzeit bis zur Gegenwart
Wie leistungsfähig ist der klassische, auf Thomas Morus zurückgehende Utopiebegriff im Vergleich zu anderen Ansätzen? Wodurch unterscheidet er sich von dem in der Frühen Neuzeit hegemonialen Chiliasmus? Welche sozio-politischen Alternativen zeigt er gegenüber dem aristotelischen und dem von Hobbes geprägten individualistischen Gesellschaftsbild auf? Wie reagiert das utopische Denken auf die Epoche der Aufklärung und des Absolutismus? Wie wirkt es in der Architekturgeschichte auf die sozio-politische Realität Europas verändernd ein? Hinterließ es Spuren in den sozialistischen Planwirtschaften? Und kann es den Herausforderungen des transhumanistischen Ansatzes heute standhalten?
Bd. 26, 2015, 200 S., 29,90 €, br., ISBN 978-3-643-13105-8

Thomas Möbius
Russische Sozialutopien von Peter I. bis Stalin
Historische Konstellationen und Bezüge. Mit einem Vorwort von Richard Saage
Bd. 25, 2015, 770 S., 79,90 €, br., ISBN 978-3-643-13077-8

André Müller
Film und Utopie
Positionen des fiktionalen Films zwischen Gattungstraditionen und gesellschaftlichen Zukunftsdiskursen
Bd. 24, 2010, 352 S., 34,90 €, br., ISBN 978-3-643-10878-4

Richard Saage
Utopische Horizonte
Zwischen historischer Entwicklung und aktuellem Geltungsanspruch
Bd. 23, 2010, 192 S., 29,90 €, br., ISBN 978-3-643-10596-7

LIT Verlag Berlin – Münster – Wien – Zürich – London
Auslieferung Deutschland / Österreich / Schweiz: siehe Impressumsseite

Ethik in der Praxis/Practical Ethics

Studien/Studies

hrsg. von Ilhan Ilkilic (Universität Istanbul), Arnd T. May (Erfurt), Amir Muzur (Universität Rijeka), Hans-Martin Sass (Universität Bochum/Georgetown University Washington), Martin Woesler (Universität Witten/Herdecke)

Martin Woesler; Hans-Martin Sass (Eds.)

Medicine and Ethics in Times of Corona

Albert Camus in *Le Peste* (1947) describes how a plague of 1849 effects and kills not only people but changes societies, values, technologies, businesses. The global Corona pandemic of 2019f has not come to an end and a cure is not in sight. Countries set aside civil and basic human rights. The pandemic brought about triage, changes in employment, social contacts, and schooling. Families and friends cannot get together, visiting the sick, nor attending funeral. Is this pestilence a cultural, economic and political disease? What impact does the pandemic have on our global networks of commerce and communication? How do different countries respond to the challenge? What ethical questions do people face in this crisis? Martin Woesler and Hans-Martin Sass have collected over 25 diverse, sometimes controversial answers from over 15 countries.

vol. 47, 2020, ca. 360 pp., ca. 49,90 €, br., ISBN-CH 978-3-643-91320-3

Arnd T. May; Barbara Seehase

Advance Care Planning (ACP) in der Eingliederungshilfe

Grundlagen und Praxis zur gesundheitlichen Versorgungsplanung (SGB V §132 g)

Bd. 44, 2020, ca. 120 S., ca. 39,00 €, br., ISBN 978-3-643-14292-4

Iva Rinčić; Amir Muzur

Fritz Jahr and the Emergence of European Bioethics

The book presents the results of a long research into the life and work of the German theologian and teacher Fritz Jahr (1895 – 1953) from Halle an der Saale, who was the first to use the term "bioethics", as early as 1926. It is a revised history of bioethics with an overview of all 22 of Jahr's known published papers. The analysis follows the diffusion after 1997 of the discovery of Fritz Jahr worldwide and particularly the contribution of Croatian bioethicists to it.

Bd. 43, 2019, 154 S., 34,90 €, br., ISBN 978-3-643-91134-6

Iva Rinčić; Amir Muzur

Van Rensselaer Potter and His Place in the History of Bioethics

Van Rensselaer Potter (1911 – 2001), the biochemist-oncologist of University of Wisconsin-Madison, was long been related to the invention of the term "bioethics". Even today, knowing that the German theologian Fritz Jahr (1895 – 1953) is to be credited for this invention, Potter's ideas do not lose on their importance, primarily for his opposition to a bioethics narrowed down onto biomedical issues. The book represents the first monograph on Potter's life and work worldwide, telling a fascinating story about a concerned top scientist and humanist.

Bd. 42, 2019, 126 S., 29,90 €, br., ISBN 978-3-643-91133-9

Tatjana Grützmann

Interkulturelle Kompetenz in der klinisch-ethischen Praxis

Kultursensible Ansätze zum Umgang mit interkulturellen Situationen in der Klinischen Ethikberatung

Aufgrund von Migrationsprozessen, individuellen Lebenskonzepten und multikulturellen Behandlungsteams erleben Mitarbeiter im Gesundheitswesen eine zunehmende kulturelle Diversität und damit verbunden interkulturelle Konfliktsituationen. Anhand von Fallbeispielen werden Lösungswege aufgezeigt und praxisorientierte Techniken zum professionellen Umgang mit derartigen Situationen im klinisch-ethischen Kontext vermittelt. Ansätze für eine kultursensible Ethikberatung, strukturelle Maßnahmen sowie Interkulturelle Kompetenz für Klinikmitarbeiter werden thematisiert und Experten im Rahmen von Interviews hierzu befragt.

Bd. 41, 2016, 244 S., 34,90 €, br., ISBN 978-3-643-13489-9

LIT Verlag Berlin – Münster – Wien – Zürich – London

Auslieferung Deutschland / Österreich / Schweiz: siehe Impressumsseite

Hans-Martin Sass
Cultures in Bioethics
LIT

Ethik in der Praxis/Practical Ethics

Materialien/Documentation

hrsg. von Prof. Dr. Hans-Martin Sass (Universität Bochum/Georgetown University Washington)
Schriftleitung: Dr. Arnd T. May

Barbara Seehase; Arnd T. May

Ich bestimme selbst! Das ist mir wichtig.

Wünsche für die letzte Lebensphase mit Patienten-Verfügung in leichter Sprache

Dieses Instrument in Leichter Sprache mit Bildmaterial eignet sich für die gesundheitliche Versorgungsplanung (GVP/ACP) für die letzte Lebensphase gemäß §132g SGB V speziell in Einrichtungen der Eingliederungshilfe. Menschen mit Behinderung werden bei ihrer individuellen Entscheidungsfindung zu ihrer pflegerisch-medizinischen Versorgung barrierefrei unterstützt. Grundlegend sind Aussagen der Klienten zu ihren Wünschen im Leben.

In schwerer Krankheit garantiert die Berücksichtigung dieser Wünsche Lebensqualität. Eine Patientenverfügung in Leichter Sprache ist enthalten.

Bd. 17, 2019, 40 S., 9,90 €, br., ISBN 978-3-643-14291-7

Hou Cai

The Guodian Bamboo Slips Lao Zi

English and Chinese Edition. Edited by Irene M Miller and Hans-Martin Sass

The 85 Lao Zi bamboo slips from around 300 B. C. E. are the earliest texts of what later became known as the 'Tao Te King'. They contain also the until now unknown Taoist narrative of Creation 'Great One gave Birth to Water'. These texts are very original and not yet intermingled with Confucian philosophy, governance, or ethics.

These, in 1993 discovered Bamboo Slips were translated by Professor Hou Cai initially into German. This English translation presents the Tao Bamboo Slips in modern simplified Chinese characters, with commentaries and a comparison of the modern Chinese version to the old characters. This bilingual Chinese-English publication is a contribution to the crosscultural visions and values of the New Silk Road of the 21st century.

Bd. 16, 2017, 142 S., 39,90 €, br., ISBN 978-3-643-90898-8

Fritz Jahr

Essays in Bioethics 1924 – 1948

Edited and translated by Irene M. Miller and Hans-Martin Sass

FRITZ JAHR (1895-1953), a Protestant theologian in Halle an der Saale, Germany, coined the term BIOETHICS in 1926 and defined the BIOETHICAL IMPERATIVE:

"Respect every living being on principle as an end in itself and treat it, if possible, as such". In critical dialogue with Kant's Categorical Imperative he develops the concept of modern situational bioethics. These 22 articles, written between 1924 and 1948, cover issues of ethics towards animals, plants and environments, also the ethics of social interactions with all forms of life.

The essays are of current and historical interest and serve as a guide to future global and integrated bioethics.

Bd. 15, 2013, 136 S., 29,90 €, gb., ISBN 978-3-643-90337-2

Fritz Jahr

Aufsätze zur Bioethik 1924 – 1948

Werkausgabe. Herausgegeben von Arnd T. May und Hans-Martin Sass

FRITZ JAHR (1895 – 1953), evangelischer Pastor in Halle an der Saale, prägt zuerst 1926 und dann prominenter 1927 den Begriff BIO-ETHIK in einem Leitartikel in der Zeitschrift „Kosmos" und formuliert als BIOETHISCHEN IMPERATIV: „Achte jedes Lebewesen grundsätzlich als einen Selbstzweck und behandle es nach Möglichkeit als solchen!" Er entwickelt damit in kritischer Auseinandersetzung mit dem Kategorischen Imperativ von Kant das Konzept einer situativen und abwägenden Ethik und den Rahmen für eine künftige integrative und globale Bioethik. Die Sammlung der zwischen 1924 und 1948 in verstreuten wissenschaftlichen, theologischen und ethischen Zeitschriften erschienenen Aufsätze von Fritz Jahr beleuchtet nicht nur die historische Entwicklung der Bioethik, sondern will auch zur Weiterentwicklung einer integrativen und globalen Bioethik beitragen.

Bd. 14, 2. Aufl. 2013, 160 S., 24,90 €, gb., ISBN 978-3-643-12137-0

LIT Verlag Berlin – Münster – Wien – Zürich – London

Auslieferung Deutschland / Österreich / Schweiz: siehe Impressumsseite